Creating Your O

Want to try drawing your own pixel desi̲ ̲ ̲ ̲ ̲ ̲ ̲ ̲ ̲ ̲
grids found throughout this book to give it a shot. If you're not sure
where to start, check out the examples on the following pages. You
can create anything you want using pixels! If it's still a little tricky, try
starting out with color variations. The same configuration of pixels
can look completely different depending on how you color in the
blocks. So, you can repeat the same basic outline over and over and
change the look of your design by coloring it differently. Use the blank
pixel grids to experiment with different designs until you come up
with something you like. Try creating different facial expressions, hair,
clothes, or accessories for your pixel art pieces. There are prompts
that accompany each grid to get your imagination going, or come up
with something all on your own! Have fun experimenting!

Eyes

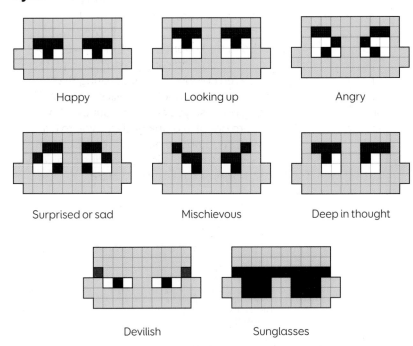

Happy

Looking up

Angry

Surprised or sad

Mischievous

Deep in thought

Devilish

Sunglasses

Mouths

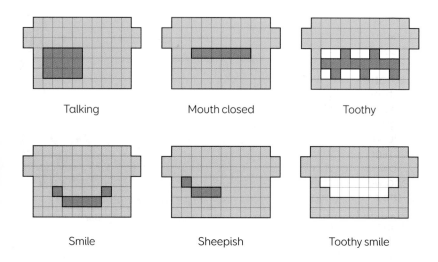

Talking

Mouth closed

Toothy

Smile

Sheepish

Toothy smile

Accessories

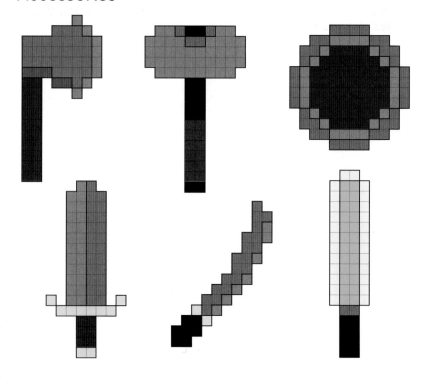

Color Tips

There's a lot you can learn from the color wheel, like colors opposite one another are complements and naturally go well together. Colors next to each other (analogous), like green/yellow/orange or blue/purple/red, also look nice. Warm colors (yellow, orange, red) blend well together, as do the cool colors (green, blue, purple). Warm colors will pop off of cool colors, grabbing your attention.

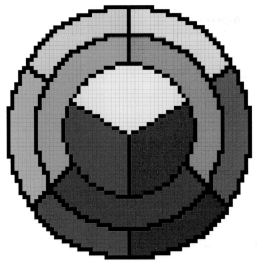

For pixel art, it is fun to experiment with analogous colors, and tints and shades of colors. Tints are progressively lighter versions of a color, and shades are progressively darker versions. For example, pink is a tint of red, and burgundy is a shade. When you color your pixel art, you can create the illusion of shading by using progressively lighter or darker analogous colors next to one another, or tints and shades of the same color.

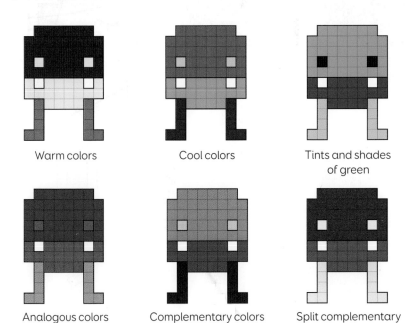

Warm colors

Cool colors

Tints and shades of green

Analogous colors

Complementary colors

Split complementary colors

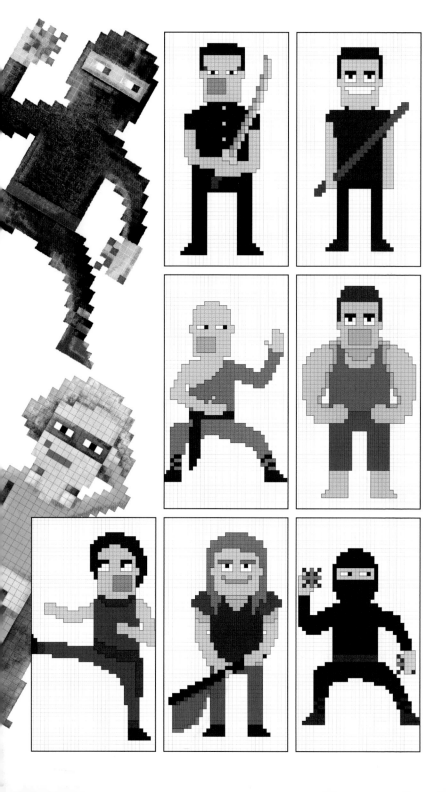

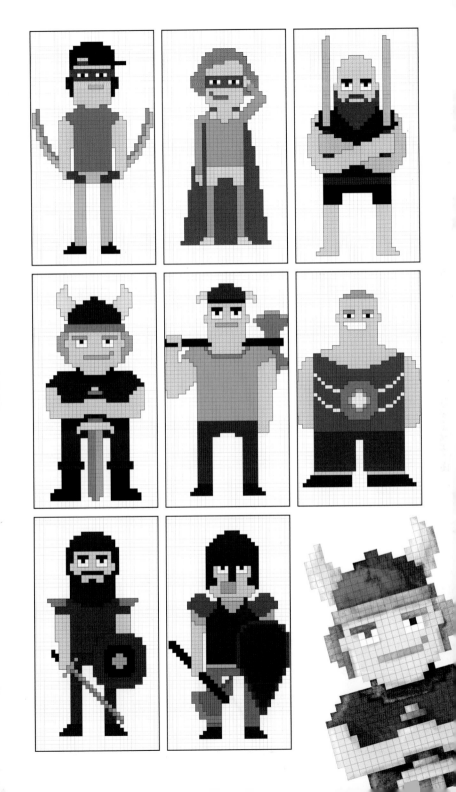

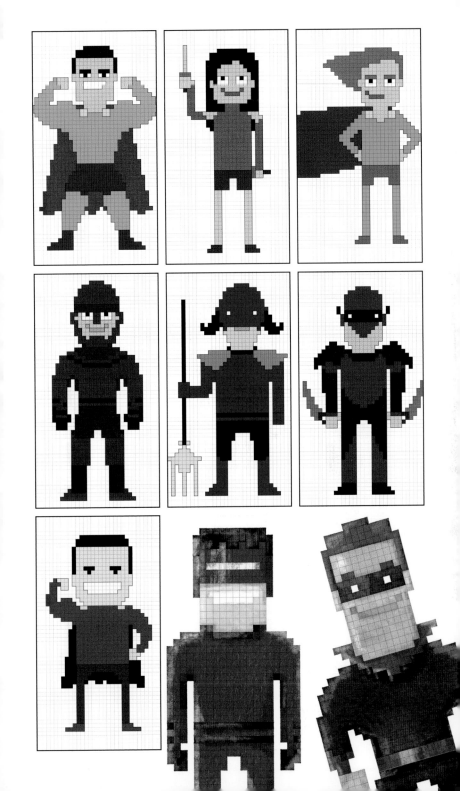

Life doesn't give us purpose.
We give life purpose.

–The Flash

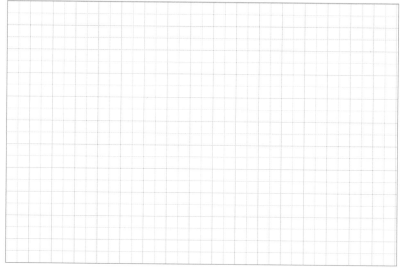

Try designing a second sword for this warrior.

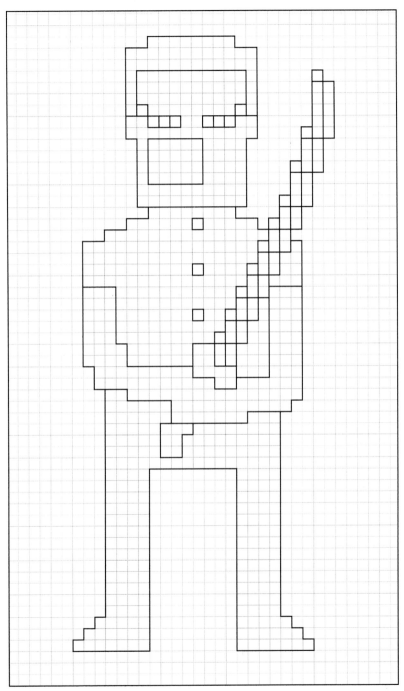

© Dmitrii Vlasov

May the force be with you.

–Star Wars Episode IV: A New Hope

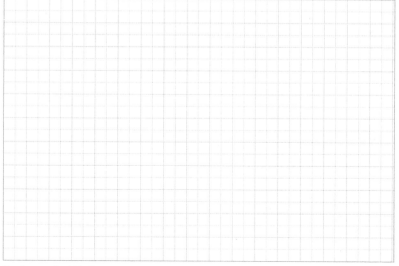

Design a pixel Yoda.

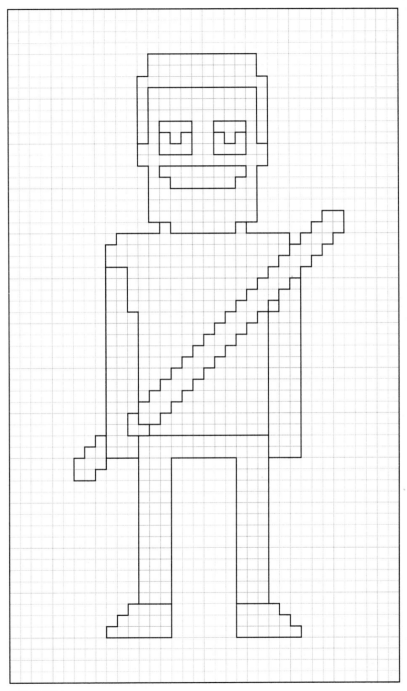

It matters not what someone is born,
but what they grow to be.

–J. K. Rowling, *Harry Potter and the Goblet of Fire*

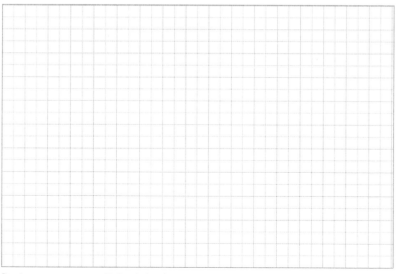

Design your own martial arts badge.

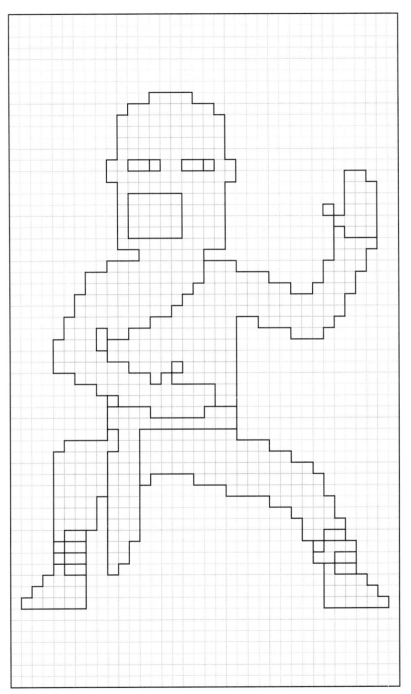

A true hero isn't measured by
the size of his strength, but by the
strength of his heart.

–Zeus, *Hercules*

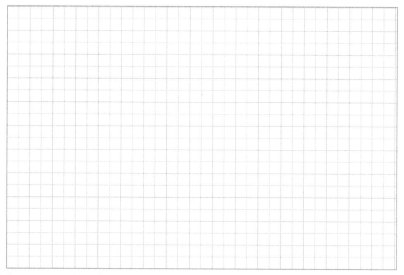

Create something for this strong man to lift.

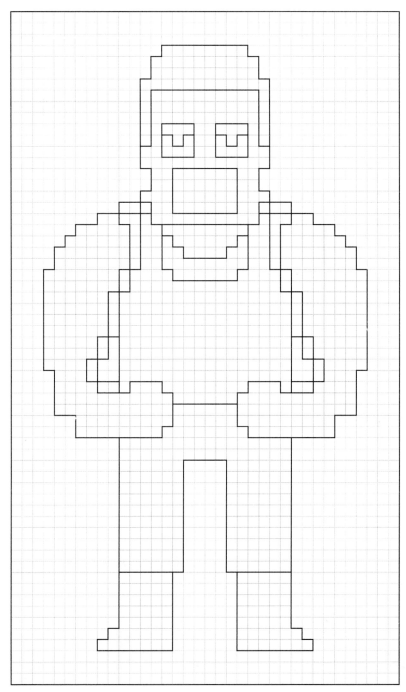

© Dmitrii Vlasov

The future is worth it.
All the pain.
All the tears.
The future is worth the fight.

–Martian Manhunter

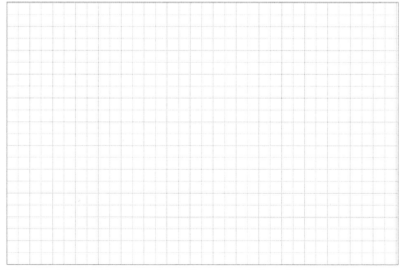

Find a cool Asian letter character and create a pixel version here.

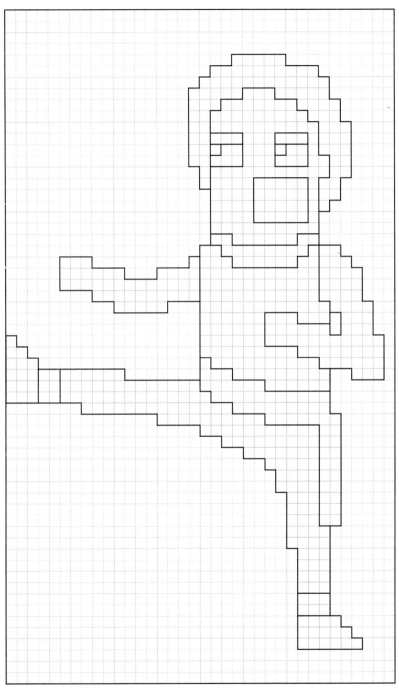

We are what we believe we are.

–Unknown

Try changing up this character's hairstyle.

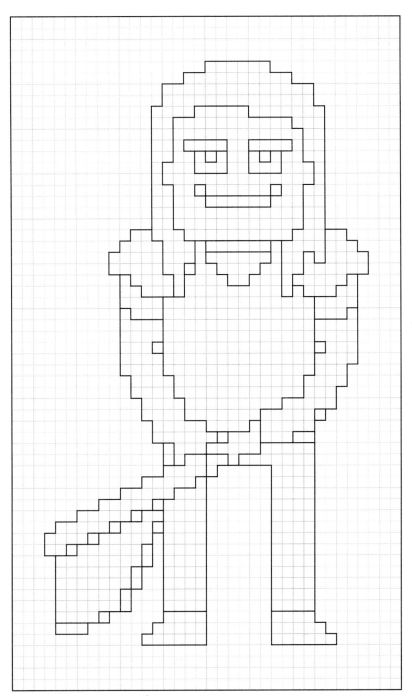

© Dmitrii Vlasov

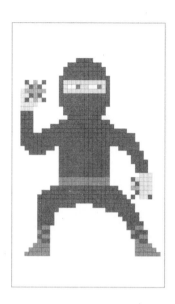

A hero does good for good, not for glory.

–Unknown

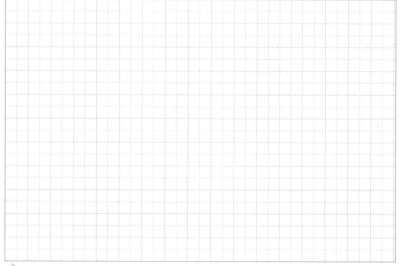

Design some cool ninja throwing stars.

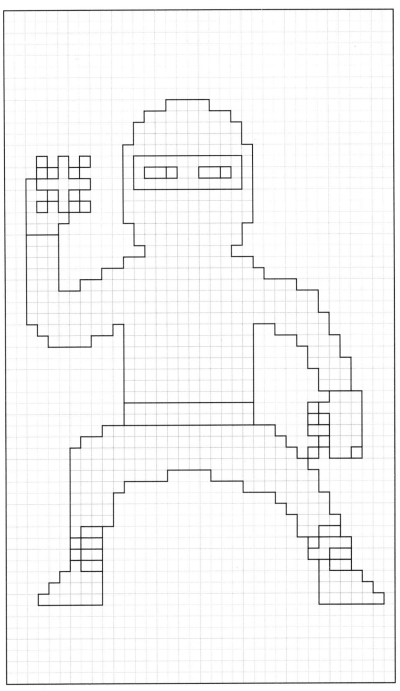

A hero is somebody who voluntarily walks into the unknown.

–Tom Hanks

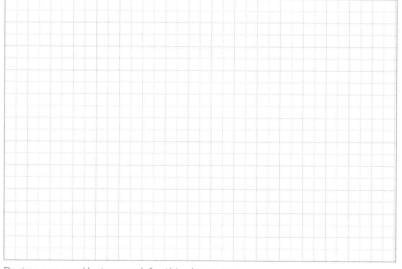

Design a second hat or mask for this character.

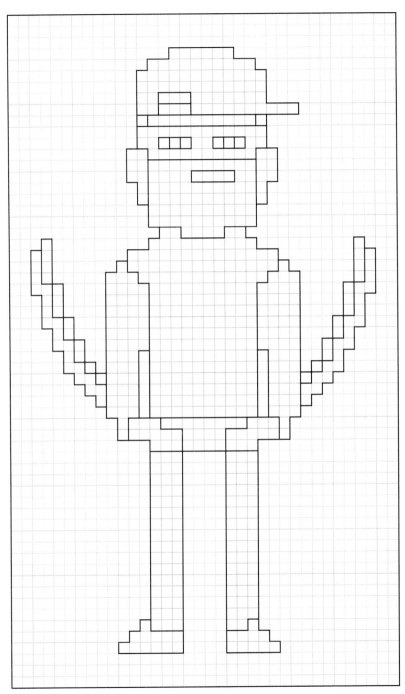

© Dmitrii Vlasov

There is a superhero inside all of us.
We just need the courage to put
on the cape.

–Unknown

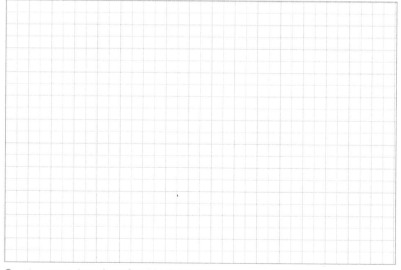

Create a superhero logo for this character.

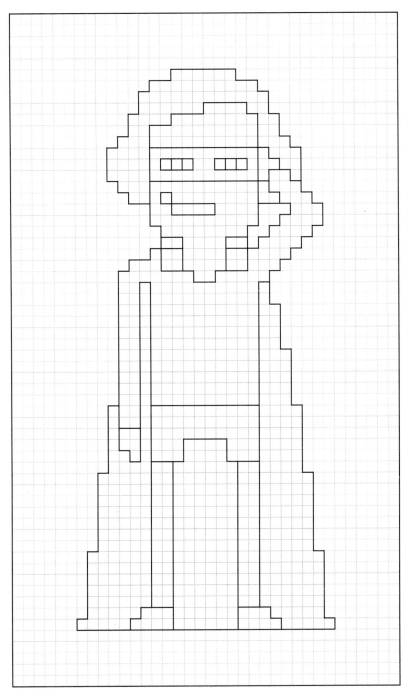

Heroes are made by the paths
they choose, not the powers they
are graced with.

–Brodi Ashton, *Everneath*

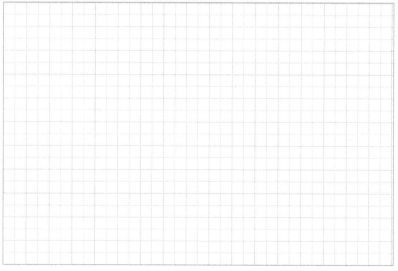

Try changing up this character's beard, or give him some hair.

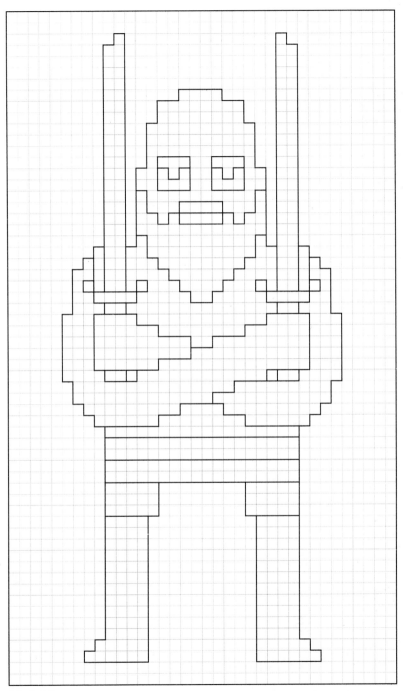

© Dmitrii Vlasov

Some are born great,
some achieve greatness,
and some have greatness
thrust upon them.

–William Shakespeare, *Twelfth Night*

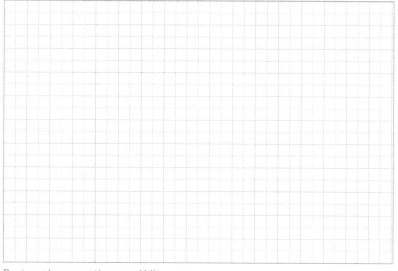

Design a hero-worthy sword hilt.

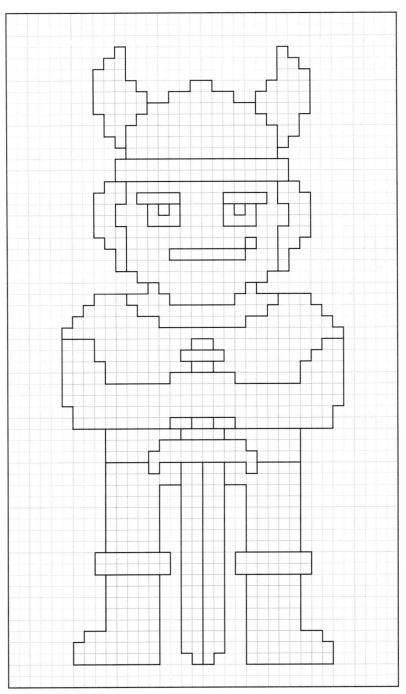

© Dmitrii Vlasov

There is nothing noble in being
superior to your fellow man; true nobility
is being superior to your former self.

–Ernest Hemingway

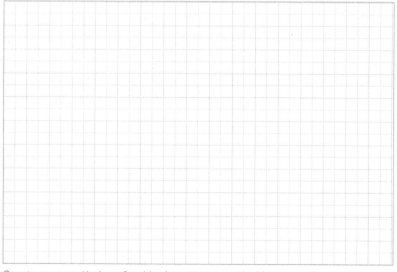

Create a second helmet for this character, or make him a sword.

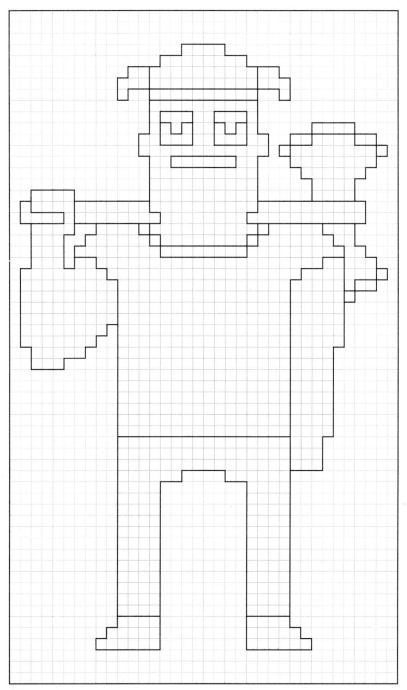

© Dmitrii Vlasov

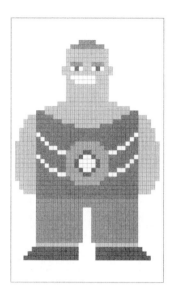

Being a hero doesn't mean
you're invincible. It just means that
you're brave enough to stand up
and do what's needed.

-Rick Riordan, *The Mark of Athena*

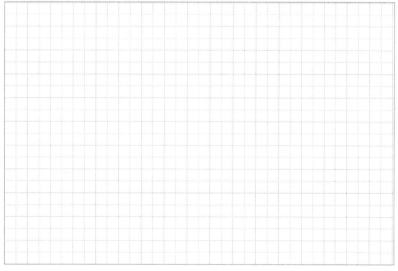

What else might this character's medal look like?

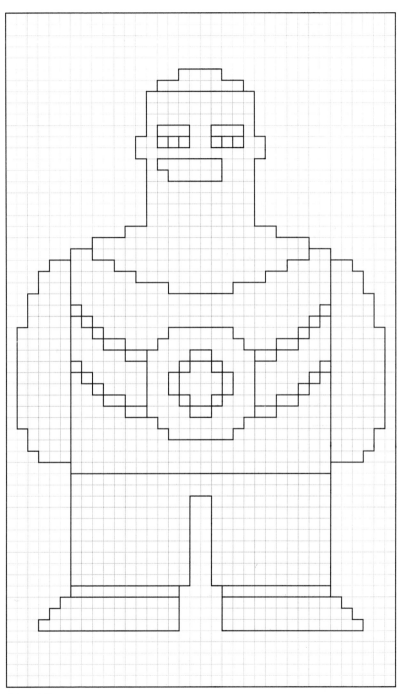

Be the kind of leader you would follow.

–Unknown

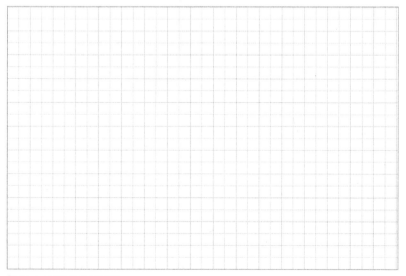

Design your own shield.

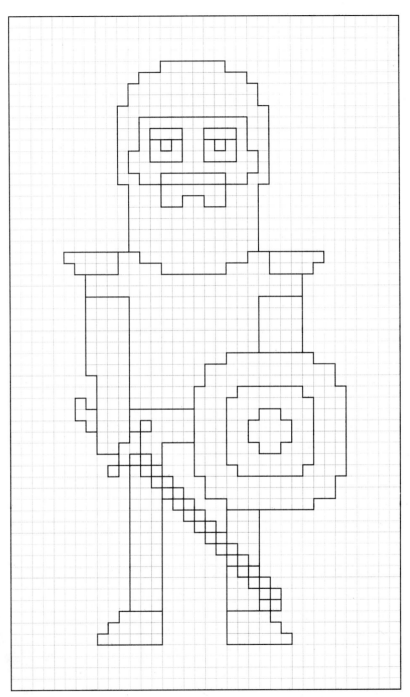

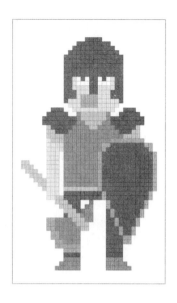

A hero is just someone who is
brave for a little bit longer.

–Unknown

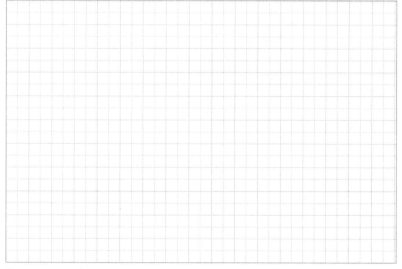

Create a crest for this character's shield and armor.

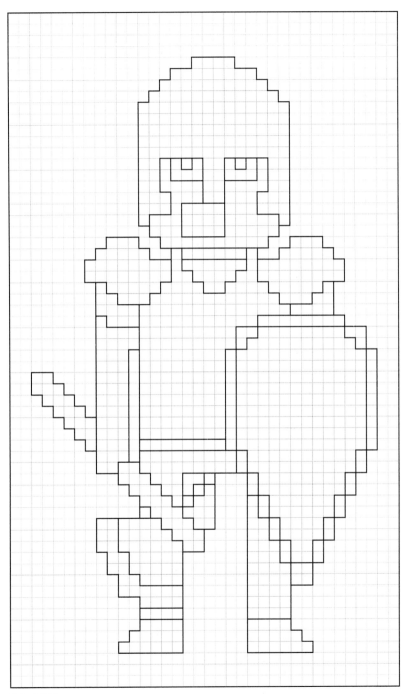

You're much stronger than you think you are. Trust me.

–Superman

Design some boxing gloves for this fit fighter.

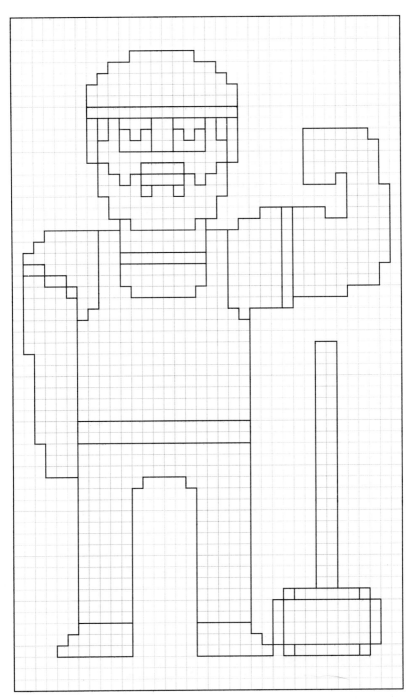

A hero is one who kindles a great light
in the world, who sets up blazing torches in
the dark streets of life for men to see by.

–Felix Adler

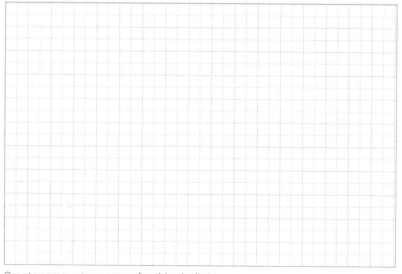

Create some unique armor for this gladiator.

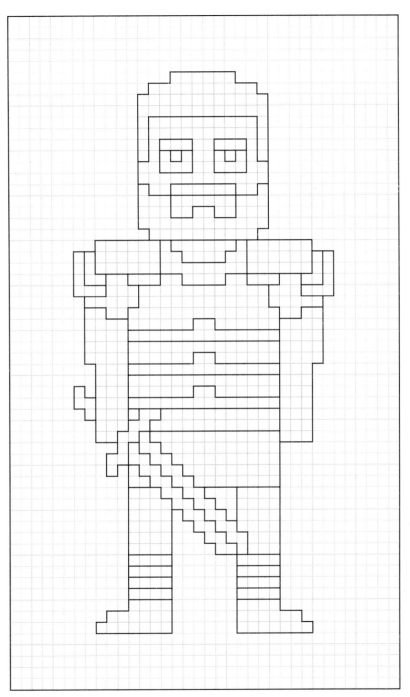

© Dmitrii Vlasov

When you've been fighting for it all your life,
You've been working every day and night,
That's how a superhero learns to fly
Every day, every hour,
Turn the pain into power.

—The Script, *Superheroes*

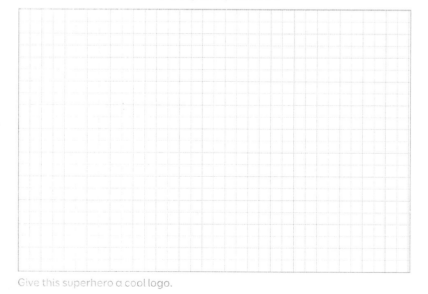

Give this superhero a cool logo.

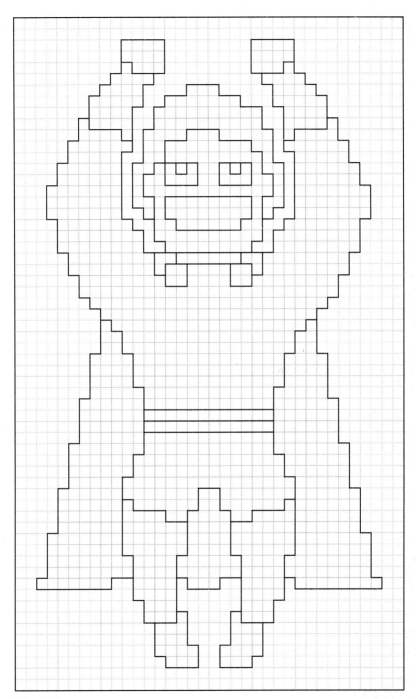

I think a hero is an ordinary individual who finds strength to persevere and endure in spite of overwhelming obstacles.

–Christopher Reeve

What else might this character's mask look like?

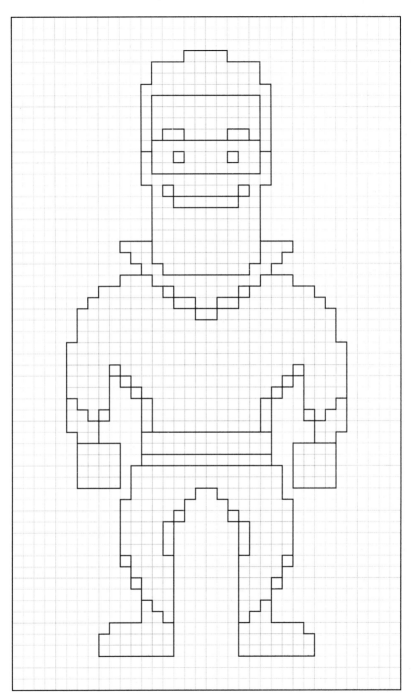

© Dmitrii Vlasov

It's not dying that you need be afraid of.
It's never having lived in the first place.

–Britt Reid, *The Green Hornet*

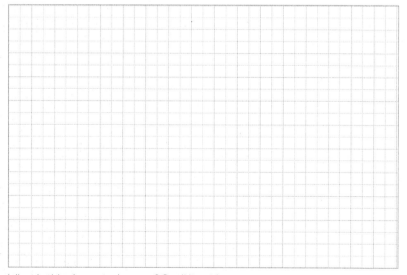

What is this character's name? Spell it out here.

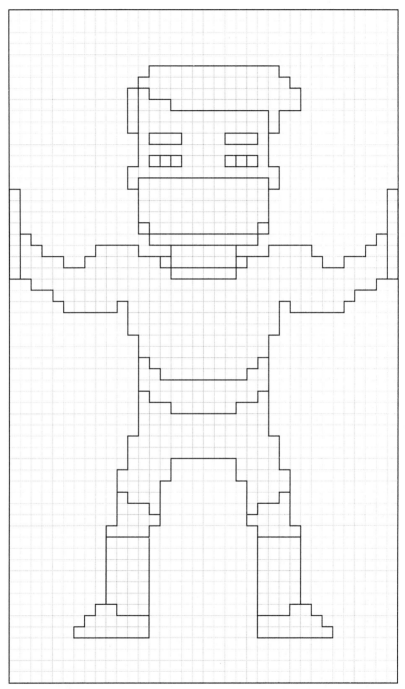

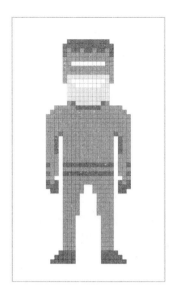

With great power comes
great responsibility.

–Uncle Ben, *Spider-Man*

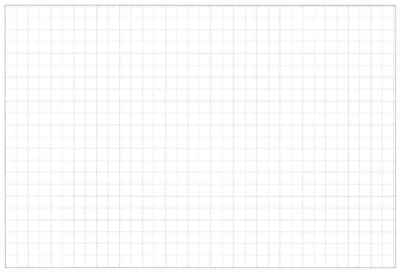

Design a plane or spaceship for this character to fly.

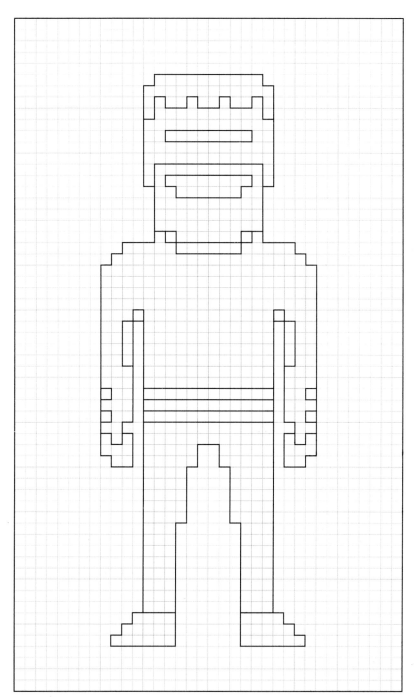

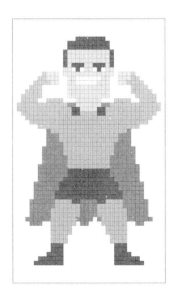

The strength of this country
isn't in buildings of brick and steel.
It's in the hearts of those who have
sworn to fight for its freedom.

–Captain America

Design a cool superhero cape.

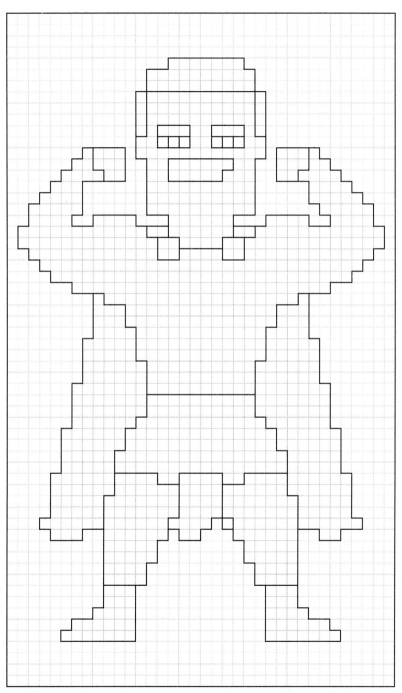

© Dmitrii Vlasov

You're going to make a difference.
A lot of times it won't be huge,
it won't be visible even. But it
will matter just the same.

–Unknown

Try changing up this character's hair.

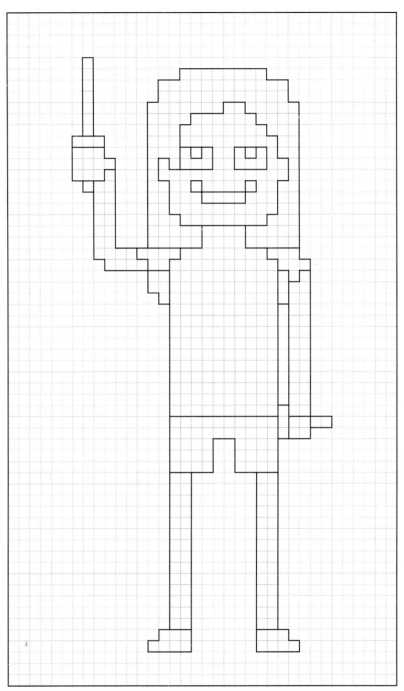

© Dmitrii Vlasov

You'll never know if you can fly unless
you take the risk of falling.

–Nightwing

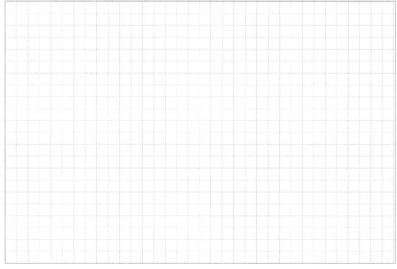

Create a city building for this character to leap over.

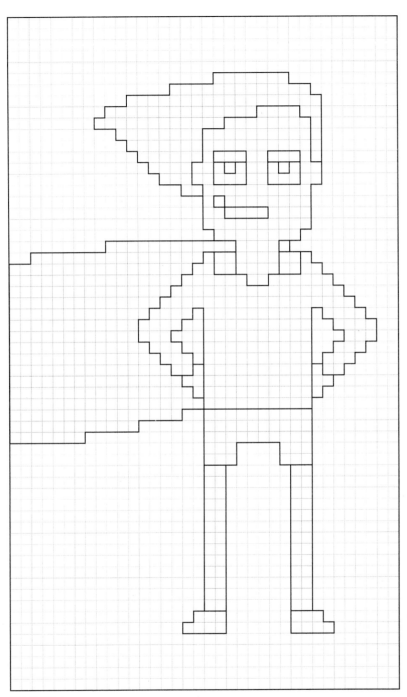

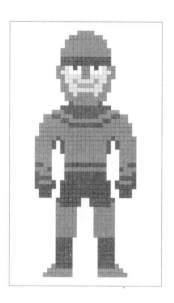

I think that we all do heroic things,
but hero is not a noun, it's a verb.

-Robert Downey, Jr.

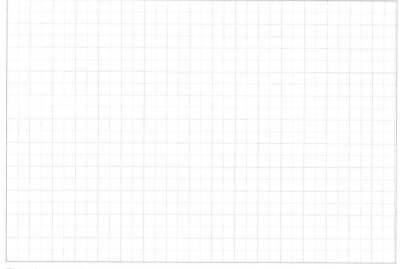

This character has a cool suit. What other gadgets might he need?

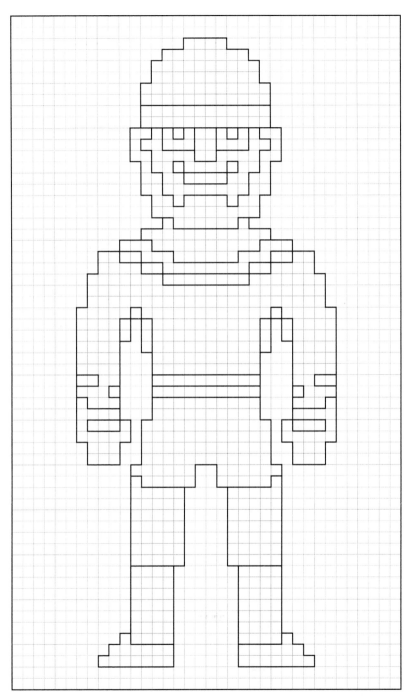

© Dmitrii Vlasov

So many of our dreams at first seem impossible, then they seem improbable, and then, when we summon the will, they soon become inevitable.

–Christopher Reeve

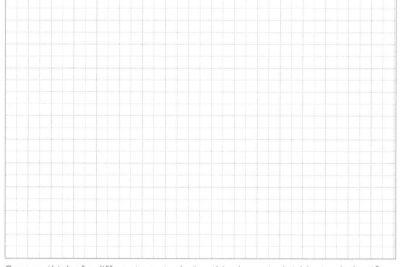

Can you think of a different way to design this character's trident or helmet?

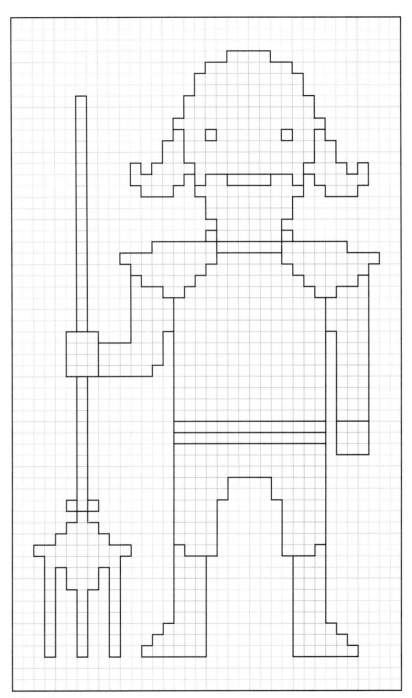

© Dmitrii Vlasov

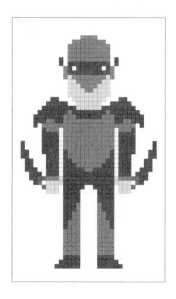

It's not who I am underneath,
but what I do that defines me.

–Batman, *Batman Begins*

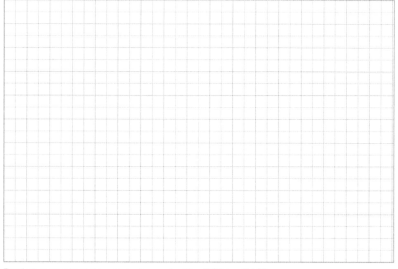

Design a comic strip onomatopoeia, like POW or ZAP!

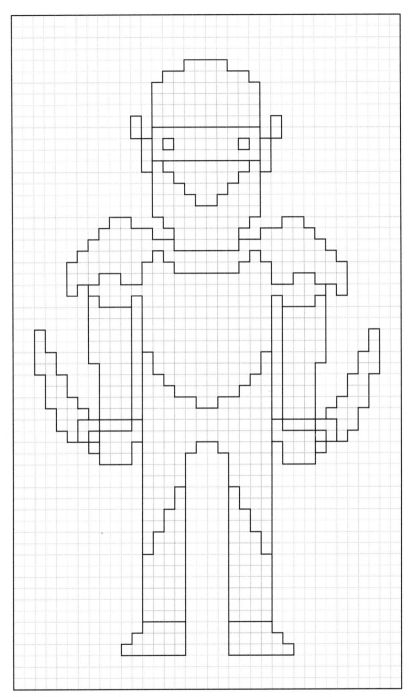

© Dmitrii Vlasov

You only have your thoughts
and dreams ahead of you.
You are someone.
You mean something.

–Batman

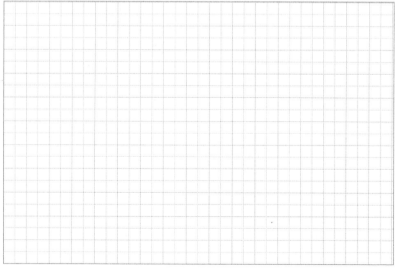

Design a telephone booth for this character to change in.

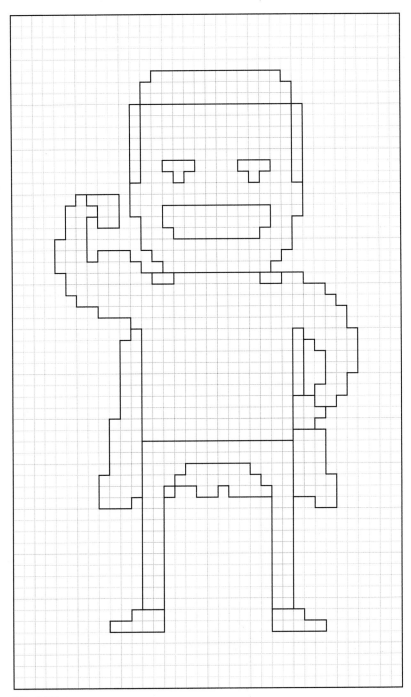

© Dmitrii Vlasov

Aa Bb

Cc Dd

Ee Ff

Gg Hh

Ii Jj Kk

Ll Mm Nn

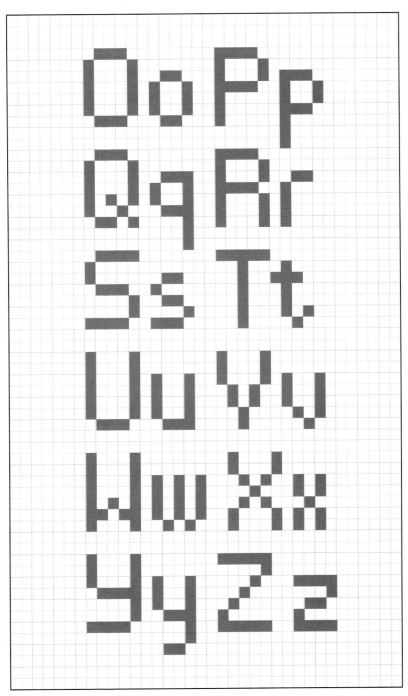

$4.99 US
$4.99 CAN
£3.99 RRP UK

Power up with
PIXELS

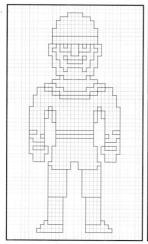

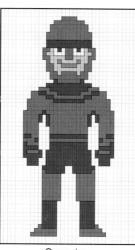

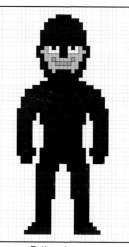

Pattern · Overview · Full-color art

Pixel Power Coloring Book features retro-cool designs for caped crusaders, knights, Jedi, warriors, ninjas, and more. Printe[d] quality, extra-thick paper that won't bleed through, it's gr[eat] in waiting rooms, on the bus, during lunchtime, or wheneve[r] break. Just use your markers, watercolors, colored pencil[s] or crayons to fill in the pixels and unleash your inner super[...]

Perfectly portable pixel art coloring

- Pixelated designs for superhero coloring fun
- Caped crusaders, knights, Jedi, warriors, ninjas, and m[ore]
- Grayscale shaded examples for each illustration
- Mix-n-match gallery of bonus design elements
- Pixel alphabet for personalized words and phrases

DESIGN ORIGINALS
an Imprint of Fox Chapel Publishing
www.d-originals.com

No. 5576

ISBN: 978-1-4972-0041-8

EAN   504

9 781497 200418